GW00854401

Poems From Northern Ireland
Edited by Annabel Cook

 Young**Writers**

First published in Great Britain in 2007 by:
Young Writers
Remus House
Coltsfoot Drive
Peterborough
PE2 9JX
Telephone: 01733 890066
Website: www.youngwriters.co.uk

All Rights Reserved

© Copyright Contributors 2007

SB ISBN 978-1 84602 920 2

Foreword

Young Writers was established in 1991 and has been passionately devoted to the promotion of reading and writing in children and young adults ever since. The quest continues today. Young Writers remains as committed to the nurturing of poetic and literary talent as ever.

This year's Young Writers competition has proven as vibrant and dynamic as ever and we are delighted to present a showcase of the best poetry from across the UK and in some cases overseas. Each poem has been selected from a wealth of *Little Laureates* entries before ultimately being published in this, our sixteenth primary school poetry series.

Once again, we have been supremely impressed by the overall quality of the entries we have received. The imagination, energy and creativity which has gone into each young writer's entry made choosing the poems a challenging and often difficult but ultimately hugely rewarding task - the general high standard of the work submitted ensured this opportunity to bring their poetry to a larger appreciative audience.

We sincerely hope you are pleased with this final collection and that you will enjoy *Little Laureates Poems From Northern Ireland* for many years to come.

Contents

Abbey Primary School, Newtownards

Megan Johnston (9)	74
Alex McGowan (7)	75
Atlanta Fisher (7)	76
Madeline Kinkead (8)	77
Gemma Kane (8)	78
Laura McCreary (10)	79
Grace Warwick (10)	80
Katie Lyall (8)	81
Sophie Rowbotham (9)	82
Ashleigh Brimacombe (11)	83
Molly McLarnon (7)	84

Drumahoe Primary School, Londonderry

Sophie Windebank (11)	85
Andrew Crothers (11)	86
Lauren Hyndman (11)	87
Samara Ritchie (11)	88
Fergus Gibson (11)	89
Holly Boyd (11)	90
Jill Jeffrey (11)	91
Ethan Duddy (10)	92
Ryan Hetherington (11)	93
Rachel Montgomery (11)	94
Dylan Craig (11)	95

Glencraig Integrated Primary School, Holywood

David McIntyre (10)	96
Emma Shaw (11)	97
Harrison Ginn (11)	98
Stephanie Craig (11)	99
Christopher Wright (11)	100
Siona Davis (11)	101
Victoria Duxbury (11)	102
Jaime Anderson (11)	103
Mark Crockford (11)	104
Emily Hewitt (10)	105
Hamish Mounsey (10)	106
Hannah King (11)	107
Jamie Woods (10)	108
David Cave (11)	109
David Duff (10)	110

Kilmoyle Primary School, Ballymoney

Jonathan O'Neill (10)   111
Mark Watters (10)   112
William McCammond (10)   113
Alison Montgomery (10)   114
Dylan Greer (10)   115
Cameron Ashcroft (10)   116
Philip Richmond (11)   117
Kathie Woodrow (9)   118
James Bleakly (10)   119
Jeff Purdy (10)   120
David McKeeman (10)   121
Jacob McAlister (11)   122
Caroline Clarke (11)   123
Abbie McIlhatton (10)   124
Robynne Blair (10)   125
Emma Hartin (9)   126
Luke Watton Austin (11)   127
Matthew Steele (10)   128
Dyan Sharkey (11)   129
Charlie Hayes (9)   130
Janice Miskelly (11)   131
David Anderson (9)   132
John McLaughlin (9)   133

Laghey Primary School, Dungannon

Aoife McVeigh (10)   134

Loughries Primary School, Newtownards

Hope Bradley (11)   135
Rhys McKee (11)   136
Anna McCormick (11)   137
Jack Ritchie (11)   138
Ross Deering (11)   139
Samantha Paden (11)   140

Lourdes Primary School, Whitehead

Eamonn O'Neill (8)   141

Rathmore Primary School, Bangor

Claire Gault (11)	142
Megan Wilson (10)	143
Xantia Quail-Mease (11)	144
Darcy Richardson (11)	145
Aaron Drury (11)	146
Amy Magee (10)	147
Andrew Moore (10)	148
Colleen Magee (11)	149
Ben Crawford (11)	150
Erin Magee (11)	151
Jessica White (10)	152
Lucy Coyle (11)	153
Sarah Heath (10)	154
Jack Denny (11)	155
Melissa Lynn (11)	156
Campbell Baker (10)	157
Conor Wright (11)	158

St Colmcilles Primary School, Downpatrick

Sophie Holland (11)	159
Chloe Kelly (10)	160
Jamie Dinsdale	161
Shannon Lavery (10)	162
Michelle Blaney	163
Grainne Gleeson (11)	164
Nicole Clinton (10)	165
Niall Clinton (10)	166
Scott Stringer (11)	167
Rebecca Curran (10)	168
Natasha Fitzsimons (10)	169
Sean McGuigan (11)	170
Connie O'Shea (10)	171
Cillian Hughes	172
Thomas Leavy (11)	173

St Joseph's School, Crossgar

Ciaran McMenamin (7)	174

St Laurence O'Toole's Primary School, Belleeks

Leah McKeown (7)	175
Fainche Quinn (7)	176
Cathal Doran (7)	177
Patrick McVerry (7)	178
Ryan Kelly (7)	179
Fearghus Quinn (10)	180
P J Carroll (9)	181

St Oliver Plunkett's Primary School, Armagh

Ronan Fearon (10)	182
Aaron Hughes (11)	183
Fionntan Nixon (11)	184
Patricia McKeever (10)	185
Eoghan McAtarsney (10)	186
Sarah McCaw (11)	187
Laura Williamson (11)	188
James Bown (10)	189
John-Joe Fearon (11)	190
Kathleen Courtney (9)	191
Eimear Murray (11)	192
Conor McGlinchey (9)	193
Michael Gwynne (11)	194
Chloe Hughes (10)	195

Silverstream Primary School, Greenisland

Chelsea Burrows (8)	196
Tammy-Lee Johnston (8)	197
Rhiannon McFadden (8)	198
Hannah Cardwell (8)	199
Ben Tosh (8)	200
William Gray (8)	201
Nathan Blackwood (9)	202
PJ Moth (8)	203
Abbie Johnston (7) & Noel Hartley (9)	204
Dean Cromie (9)	205
Ethan Morrow (8)	206
Amy Nicholson (8)	207
Craig Manning (8)	208

The Poems

Adoring Fans

I am ready to strut my stuff,
When I walk through piles of adoring fans
What will I do? Wave or just smile?
What will I wear?
What smile will I give?
But they all think it's great.
But you're up as a star on your own.
If I say something wrong or fall
I'm on the front of OK magazine.
My family have each other
But I have no one,
But fans.

Naomi Tyrie (10)
Abbey Primary School, Newtownards

Crackled Roses!

I can hear sounds,
Not of laughter but of screams of terror,
Very dark, can't see a thing.
I hear a crackling,
Is it the sound of the Germans shooting
Or the sound of bombs?
No it is the sound of war.
I keep on telling myself I'll live,
But I know I might not live to tell the tale.
I keep on pulling out a picture of my wife,
I am longing for home.
The sky is deep blue
And the ground is destroyed.
My shirt is torn,
Will I ever get out of this one?
Everything goes silent,
Is the war over?
I can't help thinking what to do.
I am shaking deep down in my bones, I'm old
But I'm not.
I will fight for my country and die for my country.

Terry Ewing (10)
Abbey Primary School, Newtownards

Christmas Day

Tick-tock, tick-tock
The days soar by,
Waiting for the day to come,
But not just days now but months,
The winter months have arranged with vengeance.

Nearly there, clock still ticking,
Waiting for December 25th,
One frustrating month to go,
December noticeable now,
Five days to go!

It's here! It's here!
All that waiting, it was worth it!
It's time to wait for another twelve months,
Oh no!

Owen Reeve (11)
Abbey Primary School, Newtownards

War Tears!

Children and families cry for help,
As bombs explode they whimper and yelp,
Tear after tear on a young girl's face,
The war has begun, is this the case?

Spitfires roar at the speed of sound,
Large numbers of people gather at mounds
Watching the gloominess of the sky fall down,
War isn't going to end is it my dear?

They leave their homes with guilt and fear,
Germans hold up their rifles and spears,
Glory to the Germans they would say,
Please soldiers please, please go away!

Sarah Court (11)
Abbey Primary School, Newtownards

Why? Darkness Why?

Darkness traps me
It attacks me
I'm in the world that destroyed my paradise
They think I destroyed their life
So they are here to destroy mine.

Through the night
And even the light
They want to fight
And give me a fright.

They think I'm weak with the power of nobody
Which is why they try to capture my body
They scout my house for my soul
But they are not leaving me with a hole!

Adam Miller (10)
Abbey Primary School, Newtownards

Fun With Friends

Cheerleading with friends
Running around the bends
Holding the scruffy pompom hems
Singing in our dens.

Skipping around the streets
Dancing to the beats
Playing on the sandy beach
Jumping on the seats.

Swimming in the seas
Running from the bumblebees
Climbing up the trees
Oh the bruises on our knees!

Karly McDade (11)
Abbey Primary School, Newtownards

A Great Day

After getting ready for football
Mr Cobett asks me and John to get the footballs and cones.
Mr Cobett asks us to do three laps round the playground,
Then we will do our warm-ups to get started our training.
The team is me, Josh, Luke and Ryan in one team,
The others are Alex, Ben, Mathew and Curtis.
The score is 2-1 to us, we come to the next match versus
The other team, it is 1-1, our first tie of the day.
Training ends, Mr Cobett tells us that there is
A match on Tuesday 6th February.

Kurtis McClure (10)
Abbey Primary School, Newtownards

My School

Learning from maths to art,
From toddler to smart,
Mine has to be the best of schools,
Even though there's so many rules.
The teachers are so kind to us,
Even when we make a fuss,
Different teachers every year,
Oh no, the fear,
Saying goodbye to all the teachers
And my school's beautiful features.
Even though you drive your teachers round the bend,
It's really hard at the end.

Lauren McAllister (10)
Abbey Primary School, Newtownards

Why?

Animals,
Animals are wonderful things.
God created them for a reason.
Why should we destroy these beautiful creatures,
For they help us travel to many places.
What is the reason for slaughtering them for their skin or fur?
Many beautiful animals have died
And some there are no more of.
Why?
What is the reason?
Some may harm us but that is because we harm them.
We are animals too:
So why?

Alex Barry (10)
Abbey Primary School, Newtownards

The Mountains

Alone at the top,
Looking down on my troubles,
Staring into blank nothingness,
So high, so cold, so lonely,
Snow falling gently on my head,
The mountain being covered in a white blanket,
My fingers tingle at the sound of the wind,
Silence at the top,
Just me and my thoughts.

Amber Scott (11)
Abbey Primary School, Newtownards

First Day At Secondary School

As I wander in the large black door and ask myself
What now?
I trek the dark gloomy corridors but don't know what to do.
I pass tall, scary people,
They stare, then laugh and call me names.
I do not feel good at all.
At break I ask people who look kind and ask kindly,
Can I please play?
But they just push me away.
I'm very lonely and ask myself where am I
And run away.

Marc Kinnier (10)
Abbey Primary School, Newtownards

First Day At School

As I slowly walk into Abbey,
As I whisper to my mum and dad,
'I'm scared.'
They say, 'You will be alright.'
But I know in my heart I won't.
As they walk me into my classroom everyone stares,
I go and get my seat.
I look at everyone,
They look friendly.
My mum and dad leave, my heart drops,
And I pray I will make a friend.

Leah Johnston (10)
Abbey Primary School, Newtownards

Paradise

Turquoise waters
White sandy beaches
Fishes the colour of a rainbow
Every ray of the sun brings happiness to our eyes
Exotic birds gliding through the crystal skies
The sun fades, the night comes
The moon glistens on a dolphin's back
The palm trees sway in a calm night breeze
Waves crash against the sandy shore
Stars light the midnight sky
This is paradise.

Chloe McCormick (10)
Abbey Primary School, Newtownards

He'll Come For Me

He'll come for me over turquoise hills
And run till his heart's content
He'll swim over seas and rivers or climb
Till his strength is spent
The power of his enduring love can have
My heart till his days are done
For Papa is the only one
Who can have my life for rent
That man himself could be a god
For the warmth of his kiss
Can make starry skies sing
And the sun a misty shadow.

Courtenay Patterson (11)
Abbey Primary School, Newtownards

My Feelings

Nastiness
Nastiness is British racing green
It smells like bad breath
It tastes like spinach
It sounds like thunder
It feels like wet mud
It lives in Evil Town.

Happiness
Happiness is illuminous yellow
It smells of a new air freshener
It tastes like doughnuts
It sounds like laughter
It feels like a fluffy kitten.

Faith
Faith is sky-blue
It smells of strawberry milkshake
It tastes like ice cream
It sounds like angels singing
It feels like a baby rabbit.

Adam Sleith   (10)
Abbey Primary School, Newtownards

I Am Alone

Sitting, gazing at a dangerous platform,
Looking up at the thick, dull clouds of thunder.
People keep staring at me like I am dinner for them,
No one has come for me so I cry to make it go away.
Love me I scream, I will be good
And now I say I am alone.

Sitting in anger and in pain,
Gazing at the old picture of my mum.
I wonder if she is OK or is she hurt?
And no one has taken me home.

It is getting dark and it is raining,
The train station has closed,
There is no way out.
I am scared and lost,
I am scared because I am alone.

Sarah Latimer (11)
Abbey Primary School, Newtownards

Trapped!

I got to sleep at 9 o'clock,
I'm lost again in the darkness of my dream.
I can't get out of this nightmare.
I feel weak and brittle.
I cannot move.
The silent darkness surrounds me greatly,
I cannot breathe, there is no air.
I need to get out, there is no exit.
I call for help but there is no answer.
I am trapped in my nightmare.
There is no way out.

Josh McCullough (11)
Abbey Primary School, Newtownards

The Looney Tunes!

A front buck tooth
An underground roof

A hungry cat
A comfy mat

A crafty canary
A delicious berry

A daft duck
A sackful of bad luck

A porky pig
A pink wig

An eating hunk
A scary punk!

A catalogue to make me a . . .
. . . Looney tune!

Jenny Marshall (11)
Abbey Primary School, Newtownards

The Fairy Queen

There is a land
Where little creatures roam,
A bird's nest, a fox's den,
A little rabbit's home.

But you don't know
What's at the end of the narrow garden,
There are elves, pixies, fairies
And a toad that says, 'Beg your pardon!'

But the most important creature
In all of Fairy Kingdom
Is the fairy queen,
With her escort, who has the greatest wisdom.

Well, if you must know,
The fairy queen is quite pretty
And, I have a special secret, if you don't know . . .
The fairy queen is . . . me!

Samantha Meredith (11)
Abbey Primary School, Newtownards

My Sister And Brother

My sister

My sister is a pest
She is definitely not the best.

She nips
And she kicks.

She makes a mess
And her name is Jess.

She always cries
And never dies.

My brother

My brother thinks he's cool
But is just so dull.

He is good at football
But can't play basketball.

He supports Liverpool
And likes going to Blackpool.

He loves his bed
But I say he is dead.

Curtis Erwin (10)
Abbey Primary School, Newtownards

Nightmare

My worst nightmare would be,
A big lizardy snake,
Which would bite any wizard,
It would climb up a wall,
And it would be very tall,
It would eat you,
And tease you,
And spit you out,
His name would be Scout.

Aaron Craig (11)
Abbey Primary School, Newtownards

My Riddle

He's as fast as lightning,
When you see him he is quite frightening,
When he was born
He was quite torn,
But he was cute just like some fruit.

Can you guess what he is?

Clue . . . He is fast and he is spotty,
He lives in a hot place.
When he grows up he can run up to 70mph.

A: A cheetah.

Alex Jennings (11)
Abbey Primary School, Newtownards

Birthday Thank Yous

Dear Auntie,
Thank you for the lovely mouse
But it has already escaped twice.
Thank you for the yellow sweater,
At least I will find my way around.

Dear Uncle,
Thank you for the rugby ball,
I have been playing with it a lot
But I kicked it on the roof
And it burst.

Dear Gran,
Thank you for some lovely
Pairs of socks.
At least I have some stripy ones
With a toy fox.

Dear Cousin,
Thank you for the lovely book,
It will go in with my other thousand more,
I have only read 97
But I will get there eventually.

Dear Grandad,
Thank you for the lovely teeth,
I will need them when I am older
So I will store them away
Until I really need them.

Dear Brother,
Thank you for the delightful fiver,
It is better than all the rest
Of the other gifts.

Daniel Tucker (10)
Abbey Primary School, Newtownards

Hockey Is The Greatest Sport

Hockey is the greatest sport,
Nothing compares to it,
It's not like any other sort.

Some people may not agree,
They might prefer
Football or squash.

But if you ask me,
I think it is the best!

It is so challenging and fun,
You get really competitive as well,
Hockey is the greatest sport!

Ashleigh Kennedy (11)
Abbey Primary School, Newtownards

The Things I Would Love To Keep

I would love to keep . . .
The helium of a vast balloon
The wealth of a prince
The sparkle of a diamond.

I would love to keep . . .
The taste of a sour lemon
The stillness of a painting
A pinch of the universe.

I would love to keep . . .
The wing of an elephant
The will of my grandparents
The gentleness of God.

I would love to keep . . .
The giggle from a horse
The neigh of a human
The tick-tock of my heart.

I would store these things
In a secret box that I can
Ice skate in and feel happy in.

Clare McIntyre (10)
Abbey Primary School, Newtownards

Not Today And Not Tomorrow

Christmas time is a jolly time
Buying presents for everyone
Spending a lot of money
Trying to make people happy
Because you know what's coming next
Ain't gonna be too jolly
In January the day comes too soon
And tells you you have to pay the price for all the Christmas shopping
Because no cheque has come today
And probably not tomorrow
So we all weep in sorrow
Because no cheque has come today
And probably not tomorrow.

Luke Humphreys (10)
Abbey Primary School, Newtownards

Africa, Africa

Such a warm continent, Africa, Africa.
Cancer tropics and Capricorn tropics, Africa, Africa.
Green lands and deserts, Africa, Africa.
Kenya, Morocco and many more, Africa, Africa.
Hot because of the lack of rain, Africa, Africa.
Poor people, homeless people, Africa, Africa.
No Christmas, no Easter, Africa, Africa.
Hungry people, Africa, Africa.
We waste so much, Africa, Africa.
We care so little, Africa, Africa.
We should give, Africa, Africa.
We should care, Africa, Africa.
Sorry we are selfish, Africa, Africa.
Sahara and rainforest, Africa, Africa.
Victoria Falls and Lake Volta, Africa, Africa.
Lake Chad and Lake Malawi, Africa, Africa.
Lake Tanganyika, Africa, Africa.
Indian Ocean and Atlantic Ocean, Africa, Africa.
Beside is the Mediterranean, Africa, Africa.
Elephants of Kenya, Africa, Africa.
Gorillas of Rwanda, Africa, Africa.
Carvings made of ebony, Africa, Africa.
Papyrus reed along River Nile, Africa, Africa.
Lagos, Niger, Africa, Africa.
Casablanca, Morocco, Africa, Africa.
We should care more for Africa, Africa,
Africa, Africa, Africa, Africa.

Jasmine Scott (10)
Abbey Primary School, Newtownards

What Am I?

You find me on a track.
You find me in the wild.
You get me in different colours.
What am I?

You can ride on my back.
I am very fast.
I race with my kind.
What am I?

You can keep me if you have money.
You can keep me in a stable.
You can keep me in a farm.
What am I?

You feed me apples.
You feed me hay.
You feed me carrots.
What am I?

You can brush my hair.
You can tie it up.
You make me pretty.
What am I?

If you feed me sugar cubes
I will get very fat,
But when you give me one or two
I will be cool with you.
What am I?

I wear a saddle.
I have hooves.
I do cool tricks
And if you're behind me
You'll do no tricks.
What am I?
I am a horse.

Georgina Turner (10)
Abbey Primary School, Newtownards

The Magic Box

(Based on 'Magic Box' by Kit Wright)

I will put in the box . . .
The taste of melted chocolate,
The looks of the beautiful teacher,
The heart of a melted snowman.

I will put in the box . . .
A teaspoon of sadness,
A heart full of happiness,
The love of my mum.

I will put in the box . . .
The teeth of an ancient king,
The wisdom of a wise man,
The love of a dad.

I will put in the box . . .
The kindness of Mrs Boyle,
A heart full of joy,
A kiss from my brother.

My box is made from ice, silver and blue,
With a sun on the top and joy in the corners.
The hinges are two toes of a dragon.

I shall fly my box into the big blue sky,
Then land on the beach of Tenerife,
The sand, the colour of the bright sun.

Courteney Quinn (10)
Abbey Primary School, Newtownards

A Riddle

She is new to our school,
She likes to keep it cool,
But stick to school rules.
She comes to school tournaments,
And cheers us on,
We're lucky she's here,
Or our school would be chaos.
She says no running in the corridors
Or no talking while eating
And many more good rules!
She is nice to the wee ones
But sometimes fierce to the big ones!
She has her own office to rule the school.
Guess who she is?

Our principal.

Phoebe Leung (11)
Abbey Primary School, Newtownards

Lamborghini

The Lamborghini is a bull,
It's a bull because of the speed
And its strength,
It can come in lots of colours.

Black and white are the best,
Doesn't need pimping,
It's got the best parts ever,
The performance is brill.

Everything is at the top,
I like the car because it's fast,
It's like lightning in the sky,
It just flies past all the cars.

It always wins the races
At the end,
I show off
By drifting and hydraulics.

Jason Bickerstaff (11)
Abbey Primary School, Newtownards

The Magic Box

(Based on 'Magic Box' by Kit Wright)

I will put in the box . . .
The neck of a giraffe,
The trunk of an elephant,
The air of a red balloon.

I will put in the box . . .
The taste of a Galaxy chocolate bar,
The smell of fish,
A hair from God's head.

I will put in the box . . .
The teeth of an ancient uncle,
The rays of the yellow sun,
A dinosaur bone.

I will put in the box . . .
The noise of an F1 car,
The hiss of a snake,
The colours of a rainbow.

My box is made of gold and silver
And the leaf of the last tree.

I will swim the Atlantic with my box
And end on a sandy beach.

Andrew Scott (10)
Abbey Primary School, Newtownards

The Magic Box

(Based on 'Magic Box' by Kit Wright)

The scent of newly cut daffodils,
The sound of a horse galloping
And the feel of the fur of a dog.

I will put in the box . . .
The taste of soft brown Galaxy chocolate,
The luckiness of winning a million pounds,
The feeling of eating a fat, long, juicy slug.

I will put in the box . . .
The sound of a loud, rainy storm,
The excitement of opening your Christmas presents,
The taste of freshly squeezed orange juice.

I will put in the box . . .
The fear of going on a roller coaster that doesn't go forward,
The sound of a car engine,
The sight of seeing a pig fly.

My box is made of strong, shiny steel
With the moon and sun stuck on.
My box is sealed with a baby's slabbers
Which will glue it closed.

I will bury my box in a deep, deep hole underground
Where it will stay forever and ever until I dig it out
And find my secrets again.

Rebecca Cully (10)
Abbey Primary School, Newtownards

The Magic Box

(Based on 'Magic Box' by Kit Wright)

I will put in the box . . .
Feelings of a pig,
A sound of a woodpecker
And a Victorian kitchen.

I will put in the box . . .
The taste of a turkey,
A spot of air from oxygen
And a thought of a boy.

I will put in the box . . .
A slurp of tea,
An elephant's trunk
And a witch's wart
From a different planet.

I will put in the box . . .
A million footballs
And three poison sticks
And a scream of a spider.

I will let all the things
I've got go free
So I can make
A new one.

It ends up
In a place
Which never ever ends.

Bethany Stevenson (10)
Abbey Primary School, Newtownards

My Family

My family's mad,
Especially my dad.
He even goes mad
If you call him Dad.

Then there's my sister, oh boy
She's a drama queen.
She thinks a tree will grow
If you throw a baked bean.

Then my mum,
Well she's kind of cool
Except . . . when she's playing pool.

My granny is kind and sweet
But she has smelly feet.

Did I mention my auntie?
Well anyway she's like a monkey,
At Christmas she travelled into town on a donkey,
I actually think she was Mary.

My dog is OK
Though he's hyper, but cute,
But the annoying thing is he eats my boot.
He has little pink bows
And he nibbles your toes.
Did I mention my dog's a boy?

I play, eat, sleep and have lots of fun,
But out of them all I'm the perfect one.

Jade Rutherford (11)
Abbey Primary School, Newtownards

The Magic Box

(Based on 'Magic Box' by Kit Wright)

I will put in the box . . .
The sounds of an abused child's cry,
A look of a bewildered giraffe
And the secrets of the unknown.

I will put in the box . . .
The taste of a wriggly worm,
A sixth sense and a black moon,
A purple goat and a green cow.

My box is fashioned from a silver spoke
Brighter than lightning,
A bronze coating darker than copper.

I shall let my friends go,
But never forget
Keep your secrets
Close from the unknown
And never tell a soul.

Brooke Beck (10)
Abbey Primary School, Newtownards

A Spring Day

I can see the bright blue sky
And cars shining lovely in the sun.

The sun shining brightly.
I see trees swing
In the sun and sky.
People in jets in the sun.
Birds sing in the sky.

People hearing the birds sing.
I smell the food
And smell the car fumes
And fly in the sky.

I feel the warm sun on my back,
I feel happy when I am out in the sun.

Desiree Gamble (10)
Abbey Primary School, Newtownards

Anger

Anger is as red as a dragon's fire.
It feels like a heart cut in half.
It is as hot as a volcano.
It is evil like the Devil.
Anger is as strong as steel.

Anger's eyes are like a fiery flame.
It is as tall as a giant.
It has a red sword and shield.
Its breath is as bad as burnt coal.
Anger can change into different shapes.

Anger has a black cloak that protects it.
It is over 1,000,000 years old.
It has scars around its forehead.
Wrinkled around its eyes.
Its hair is a horrible black.

Anger is a powerful lord.
It robs houses all night long.
People look at it and run away.
At night it uses its powers to give people nightmares.
Anger stays hidden until there is moonlight again.

Matthew Campbell (10)
Abbey Primary School, Newtownards

A Spring Day

I saw seagulls swooping in the sky
The cars gleaming
People doing their jobs
I could also see the sun shining
The sky blue as it can be.

I could hear the birds chirping away
I could hear the boiler on
I also could hear the factories working away
The cars being driven on the roadside.

I could smell food in the factory
As people walked past me I could smell perfume
I also could smell car fumes
The smell of the food was delicious.

I could feel the breeze pushing me along the road
But I still felt happy
The sun was warm on my back.

Karla Scott (10)
Abbey Primary School, Newtownards

A Spring Day

I can see the sun bright in the sky
The birds are flying in the sky
Cars whizzing around on the roads
The trees swaying side to side
People wandering about their business.

I can hear the birds sing
The boiler as loud as ever
The cars' motors are loud
Factories' machines are going
Children scream with laughter.

I can smell the food cooking
The car fumes puffing away
The smell of perfume in the air
I smell smoke of the house.

I can feel the coldness
The happiness in the air
Warm sun burning on my back
I feel the friendship
I feel the hunger in my stomach.

Matthew Hanna (11)
Abbey Primary School, Newtownards

A Spring Day

Spring is a day when daffodils shoot up.
Spring is a day when people are out.
Spring is a day that romantic people go out.
Spring is a time that people can pick daffodils for their lovers.
Spring is a time of the year that the sun is out beaming onto cars.
Spring is a time of the year when people have laughter.
Spring is day when people have picnics.
Spring is a time when you have bright green grass.
Spring is when you have rain showers instead of hailstones
crashing down.
Spring is a time when people can go out on a trip.

Joanne Moore (11)
Abbey Primary School, Newtownards

A Special Day

On this day
I don't go out and play.
I sit in the house
And try to catch a mouse.

Eddie Irvine's is the place I have to go to,
I have to go and have my party
And try not to act like a big smarty,
Hurry up Mum let's go!

When I am in the car
I ask to go to the Spar.
My dad says no,
We can't stop now we have to go.

When we got there
It was a wee bit bare,
So I went in to play
On this special day.

I passed to my dad,
His control was really bad.
I wait some time
But then they arrived.

Everyone said how long was I in bed?
Oh no! they saw my head,
Yes today was my
Birthday!

Josh Barnes (11)
Abbey Primary School, Newtownards

My Special World

My special world is filled with hope and happiness,
No fear or jealousy.
It is in everyone's heart,
You just have to search for it.

Everyone is friendly to one another,
No tears or sadness.
It has rainbows and blue skies,
Not one single grey cloud in sight.

Come and have a look in my special world,
It won't bite.
It is for children with imagination,
No adults allowed.

The opposite of my special place is simple,
It's plain and boring.
It is filled with hatred and anger,
It is called the Sinner's Land.

It is awful,
Worse than anything you can imagine.
The fights and screams,
It is full of noises and hurtful words.

It is black and gloomy,
Always rainy weather,
Crashing thunder and enormous bolts of lightning,
Not particularly nice.

This place is overcrowded,
My special world is not.
I sometimes wonder why,
Can you help me find out?

Leah Green (11)
Abbey Primary School, Newtownards

The Rainy Day

I wake up and hear rain,
I have breakfast but the rain won't stop.
Then I hear a noise, it sounds like thunder,
I wake up Mum and ask to go out.
She says no and tells me to play games.
The thunder makes me scared so I run away into my room,
In the room I hear noises which are very freaky.
It's a scary and a dark place in this house,
Something is walking in the corridor.
I hide under the bed,
My door opens but then I go out.
I go and see my window is open but it was only rain.
My mum comes out and closes the window.
The rain stops at 3 o'clock.
It is wet all over the land,
But it is fun playing in the muck.

Leon Chan (11)
Abbey Primary School, Newtownards

That Morning

I wake up and look around,
I know what day it is.
Yes, it is the day I get my results,
Oh what can it be.

I run down the stairs,
Shaking from head to toe,
I see an envelope on the chair,
I can't bear to open it.

Is it an A or is it a D?
I just don't know,
I open it slowly, ripping the envelope,
I look at the corner and there it is.

In amazement it's an A!
Suddenly I jump for joy,
The phone rings, I answer it quickly,
It's my friend, she got an A,
We scream and shout and jump about.

Later on we go for lunch,
I say to my mum oh it's all over,
Time flies, it is 10pm,
I get into bed and fall asleep,
And dream of what school I'll pick.

Monique Waycott (11)
Abbey Primary School, Newtownards

The Mysterious Woman

There once was a woman,
Who is never seen
And won't reveal her name,
Nobody's seen her for twenty years,
Not even her mum, dad and children,
On the news people are saying, 'Where is she?'
But no one knows,
People say that she could be dead,
But is she or is she not?
Well no one knows,
Maybe if we have a look,
She might be hiding in the woods,
Everyone searching everywhere,
Where is she? Oh help us please,
Then all of a sudden,
We hear a crack,
Is that her?
Yes it is,
Call an ambulance somebody please,
What's your name? As the man asks her,
Lisa, she says, oh help me please,
I want to go home please,
When she arrives, everyone shouts,
Lisa, hooray!

Shannon Weir (11)
Abbey Primary School, Newtownards

My Best Friend

My best friend has dark brown hair,
His clothes are neat and tidy,
He has brown eyes
And a bright smile.
He is smart
And kind, courteous too.
He loves animals
And wants to be a vet.
He is the most honest person
I have ever known.
He wouldn't start fights
Or try to end them,
He would ignore them
And walk away.
Do you know who he is?

When I am around him
He makes me feel happy, safe
And full of joy.
He wouldn't say a nasty word
To hurt your feelings.
He writes brilliant stories,
Poems too.
He always listens
And he would never ignore you.
He is mostly happy
But sometimes very sad.
I hope he never changes,
His name is Kyle McIlwrath.

Kurtis Scott (11)
Abbey Primary School, Newtownards

Lost In The Woods

Dark trees hidden in thick mist,
Cold breeze drifts round my shoulders,
Owls hooting, cats screeching,
Leaves crackling under my feet,
Deeper, deeper into the woods.

Eyes peering from an old tree stump,
Shivers down my spine,
Alone in deep, dark woods,
Nobody else is about,
Deeper, deeper into the woods.

Branches swaying, ready to grab me,
Bats screeching, vultures squawking,
Feet are pounding behind me,
Nowhere to go for help,
Deeper, deeper into the woods.

Shrink into a corner and cry,
Will I ever be found?
Suddenly I hear people,
Can it be my mum?
Yes! I'm free from the woods' clutches,
Now it awaits somebody else.

Amber Kelly (11)
Abbey Primary School, Newtownards

A Spring Day

I step out of the big red door,
The coldness wraps around me,
Although the sun is shining brightly in the sky
And I feel as happy as can be.

Seagulls look for leftovers in the playground,
Flying around everyone's head,
Jets in the sky taking people to different countries,
The trees swaying with the gentle breeze.

People walking around doing their jobs,
The sky is a lovely blue,
Cars parked waiting for teachers and staff,
Daffodils starting to come into bloom.

Perfume coming from pupils' bodies,
The school dinners, food getting ready to eat,
Cars zooming around,
Petrol fumes escaping from their exhausts.

Distant factories I can hear,
Birds squawk as there is no more food,
The boiler makes a loud noise
And the cars race down the road.

People moaning as we have to go back into the classroom
On this perfect spring day.

Rebecca Kenna (10)
Abbey Primary School, Newtownards

My Bestest Ever Friend

My bestest ever friend is my bestest ever friend
Who only I can see
His name is Humphrey
Humphrey is very tall
And very slim.

My bestest ever friend has dark brown hair
And eyes like hazelnuts
Humphrey is very neat but I'm a bit scruffy
He also remembers to say please and thank you
I don't sometimes but only sometimes!

My bestest ever friend likes to play games
Yesterday we played 'Dragons'
Then we climbed Mount Everest even though I'm only five
I love playing 'Dragons' with Humphrey.

My bestest ever friend and me played 'Dragons'
With monsters everywhere
And boom-boom birds flying above
Then a loud noise
Boom! A . . .

My bestest ever friend and me have to go to bed
Oh well the 'Dragons' can wait till tomorrow
Right Humphrey!

Louise Nesbitt (11)
Abbey Primary School, Newtownards

Scruffy The Dog Of Midnight

I am Scruffy and this is my story,
It is a winter's night,
It's cold and dark like all the other nights,
But this night is Scruffy's night.

I run down an alleyway and meet a cat called Tom,
I bark, prance, dance to get it off the wall,
I give in. It will never jump off the wall,
I walk on until I see a trash can,
I jump in the trash can to look for food but all that is there
Is of course rubbish.

Tom the cat is following me grinning,
It must have a cunning plan,
I jump onto the wall,
Only Tom jumps off and smiles.

I've always hated that cat, I thought as I jumped off the wall,
Finally I go down the alleyway that leads me to my friends,
But the alleyway is deserted,
Oh no I forgot tomorrow is Scruffy's night.

Kyle McIlwrath (11)
Abbey Primary School, Newtownards

Night Sky

Nothing but darkness I see up above me
I hear the trees swaying though can't see a thing
Gazing up high I see sparkles in the sky
Hoping the sun will come soon
The night-time noises keep me awake
Stars in the sky right in my face
Keeping safe but staying calm
Yet when I awake I'll see the sun in the sky.

Méabh McClurg (11)
Convent of Mercy Primary School, Downpatrick

The Lonely Lion

Behind the bars the lion stares
as people pass his cage
with curiosity and glares
that fills his heart with rage.

His thoughts turn to the way things were
when jungle was his home,
without a worry or a care,
there he was free to roam.

Niamh Campbell (10)
Convent of Mercy Primary School, Downpatrick

The Pegasus And The Fairy

See the fairy dance at night
See the Pegasus at its flight
I see their silhouette against the moonlight
What a picture they make in the sky
I wonder if the fairy dust could ever make me fly?

Catriona Gilliland (11)
Convent of Mercy Primary School, Downpatrick

The City That Never Sleeps

It's the city that never sleeps,
You won't be able to sleep a peep.

With candy canes and streets insane,
There's Broadway and highways.

There's lots of malls and the city stalls,
There's Central Park . . .
But there is so much, I love them all.

If you want to eat something without a fork,
There is a city called New York!

Emily Blaney (11)
Convent of Mercy Primary School, Downpatrick

Dancing

Dancing and lively prancing,
Salsaing and grand waltzing,
Hip hopping and cool bopping,
Cha-chaing and fun ra-raing,
Oceanish east coast swing,
And last of all the live jive.

Orla Kelly   (10)
Convent of Mercy Primary School, Downpatrick

The Plog

I sit near the bin,
I'm made of gold tin
And I'm a Plog from Pluto.

I have long, long hair
As pink as ink,
I'm a Plog from Pluto.

I don't like my arms,
They're as fat as a rat,
I'm a Plog from Pluto.

My legs are as black
As a big fat cat,
But they're also as small
As a bouncy ball,
I'm a Plog from Pluto.

My ears are as tan
As a good frying pan,
I'm a Plog from Pluto.

Laura Miskelly (10)
Convent of Mercy Primary School, Downpatrick

The Little Buzzy Bee

The buzzy little bee around my house
Will never leave me alone,
If it stings again I'll shout
Please, please go home!

Even the begging question I asked
Never worked for me,
I really, really want that bee to fly
Away from me.

Ciara Brannigan (11)
Convent of Mercy Primary School, Downpatrick

The Dog Next Door

Just when I go out the door,
The dog next door will bark and roar,
It jumps, leaps and hustles through the gate.
I'm going to be its bait!

So I get on my bike,
Cycle down the lane and round the lake
To find my nana's house and my scruffy sheepdog friend Jake.

Katie Magee (11)
Convent of Mercy Primary School, Downpatrick

Twinkle Toes

I love to watch the fairies
Who come out late at night
They love to dance and sing
Under the bright moonlight.

But then there is the special one,
I call her Twinkle Toes,
Hair so blonde,
Eyes so green,
The prettiest fairy I've ever seen.

She dances so light,
Floats so soft,
Flies so high
In the sky.

Alana Kelly (11)
Convent of Mercy Primary School, Downpatrick

My Dog Sooty

We got him as a present
A medium-sized dog lying in the kitchen
There he was when I came down for breakfast
I nearly fainted when I saw him
I ran to tickle him and hug him
I sat there all day in the kitchen to tickle my new dog
I loved him so much I didn't even remember my breakfast.

Andrew Martin (10)
Culmore Primary School, Londonderry

The Dragon Boat Race

I got inside my boat with 49 oarsmen
We waited for the gun to be shot
A drum was beating
To keep us on the right track.

We were last
The drummer beat faster and faster
We rowed faster and faster
We came second in the race.

The water was rougher
It was harder to row
Other boats were passing us
We came last again.

The drummer had given up
He thought we had lost
I kept rowing like mad
Suddenly we'd won the race.

A gust of wind had helped us
We were awarded the Dragon Boat Trophy
Another boat had sank
Some survived but others were lost.

Conor Lennon (10)
Culmore Primary School, Londonderry

PSP

My PSP is the purist milky white
It's like a handheld cloud

My PSP is a joy for me
I play it and play it even through tea

It plays music, movies and games too
The discs are like ants to me and you

That's my PSP where I spend half my time
That's my PSP and I'm out of rhyme.

Cormac O'Hagan (11)
Culmore Primary School, Londonderry

Dragon Race

Oar in hand waiting for the gun
Spectators standing on the bridge
Gun pointed in the air
Bang!

You hear the bang, the cheering begins
The dragons take off
Gliding through the water
Wings outstretched.

Other dragons begin to trail behind
But we're still flying along
Moving quickly fish stop and stare
They watch the race.

We see the end and are getting close
Crowd screaming and shouting
Cross the finish and we've won the race!

Ronan Fegan (11)
Culmore Primary School, Londonderry

Dolphins

Rubber skin from head to toe,
Fins and flippers in the flow.
Leaps from sea then down below,
Back to its sea home dolphin goes.

Babies whine, they miss their mother,
She's coming with food for the others.
They tuck in, share with each other,
While resting is their tired mother.

But lurking near in threatening danger,
A grey and white sharp-toothed stranger.
A shadow creeps over their manger,
A dolphin's squeal, away swims stranger.

Mother wakes, her babies gone,
She searches far, she searches long.
She's lost her daughter, lost her son,
For now her trio's down to one.

Eimear Kearns (11)
Culmore Primary School, Londonderry

My Mobile

My cover has beautiful butterflies
    flying through a sunset
It is a million things
    lying in your hand
It's your friends right at
    your fingertips
It is hundreds of memories
    on that little screen
It's a collection of phone dangles
    hanging there in mid-air.

Grainne McGowan (11)
Culmore Primary School, Londonderry

Animals

Cats are small, cute and cuddly.
Dogs are jumpy, they like to bark.
Rabbits are keen to get on with things.
Hamsters are little eating machines.

Horses are gentle with long tails and manes.
Chipmunks are noisy and quite a pain.
Budgies like to go cheep, cheep and cheep.
Parrots are bright coloured rainbows.

Caterpillars like to munch at lettuce leaves.
Busy bees go on long journeys for honey.
Creepy-crawlies scuttle under your feet.
Trapdoor spiders watch out for their meat.

Emma Keanie (10)
Culmore Primary School, Londonderry

Rocking

Poetry is not my thing.
Rocking like mad is my only dream.
Rocking is crazy, it gets you all hazy.
Rocking on stage, it builds up your rage.

Come on! Get that head banging.
Come on! It don't have to be rhyming.
Come on! Don't need a lucky clover.
Come on! And now the rocking is over.

Rory Anderson (10)
Culmore Primary School, Londonderry

Dragons

When dragons roar they fly and soar
Gracefully through the air,
They take pride and pleasure
In their treasure
And little jewels galore.

Their breath is smoke,
Their heart is fire,
Their eyes are filled
With wild desire.

David Prince (10)
Culmore Primary School, Londonderry

Five Best Friends

I have five best friends,
Emma, Gemma, Katey, Dearbhaile and Megan.
We met in St Columb's Park,
It was a shimmering, shining day,
The best day of my life.

A year or so later
Our friendship is stronger,
We're older now, there's been the odd fight
But whatever happens
We'll always be the best of friends.

Rachel Twells (10)
Culmore Primary School, Londonderry

They're A Family

The fresh stallion gallops round wildly,
He sees his newborn daughter and neighs proudly.
He teaches her to walk,
Then they gallop round loudly.

The sun shines upon them,
With their white coats gleaming.
They trot back to the mother,
Who is happily dreaming.

The father lies down,
He falls asleep too.
The baby looks round,
Doesn't know what to do.

It tries to sleep,
But that's no good.
It goes over to the mother,
Expecting her to know the bother.

She feeds it for a while,
Then it cuddles in by the stile.

Katey Kearns (9)
Culmore Primary School, Londonderry

Scary Wood

Once upon a scary wood
Where a scaly beast once stood
Every day it went away
It went to take a child from play

Every day and every night
The mighty beast had taken flight
One Saturday morning the beast went hunting
A human killed him, it was stunning.

Taylor Quigley (10)
Culmore Primary School, Londonderry

Bumblebee

One day I sat by a tree,
Then I saw a bumblebee.
It only had one leg
And I called it Meg.

I took it to the park
Until it went dark.
'It is too late to stay,
But we can come back another day.'

We went back to the house
Where the bee stung a mouse.
We went back to bed
And the bee slept on my head.

I woke up in the night
Then the bee had a fight.
I went back to sleep
And the bee had a weep.

Ciara Jade Gilroy (8)
Cygnet House Preparatory School, Bangor

Family

F amilies rock and wear different socks.

A ll of us sing while we go, 'Bling, bling.'

M y family is mad but they're not all that bad.

I love my family very much, they're always phoning me
to keep in touch.

L ove they say makes the world go round and that is sure
what I have found.

Y es it is a well-known fact - my family is a class act.

Megan Johnston (9)
Cygnet House Preparatory School, Bangor

Friends

I love my friends and they love me,
We play all day then go home for tea.

Hanna, Atlanta, Gemma and Anna,
I like strawberries and they like bananas.

We like blowing bubbles and playing on Heelys,
We ride our bikes and like to do wheelies.

Alex McGowan (7)
Cygnet House Preparatory School, Bangor

Poor Little Ted

Poor little Ted fell out of bed,
And found that he had a big bump on his head.
He let out a scream,
I woke from my dream
And soon made him better with cake and ice cream.

Atlanta Fisher (7)
Cygnet House Preparatory School, Bangor

The Haunted House On Smith Road

There was a haunted house
With a haunted mouse.
With skeletons and bones
And moans and groans
And a ghost that says, 'Boo!'
The witches all say, 'Whoo!'

Chains clatter,
Brains splatter,
Skeletons on the wall,
Bats in the hall,
A creaking door,
Werewolves snore.

Zombies shout,
Vampires come out,
Suck blood from Mr Flood.
He died of fright in the night!
What a sight!

Madeline Kinkead (8)
Cygnet House Preparatory School, Bangor

My Animals

My bunny is funny
When I tickle its tummy
It scampers away to hide in the hay
We'll have to play another day.

My donkey Star
Can run very far
She sings ee-haw
While lying in the straw.

My cat is fat
But I don't mind that
It eats lots of food
When it's in a good mood.

My dogs Archie, Dan, Ben and Bart
They're all very fast and they like to dart
Their coats are very furry
And it jiggles when they're in a hurry.

The fish I have are very small
They are no trouble at all
They swim around and around
And they never make a sound.

The woodland behind is full of creatures
All different shapes and sizes, some with funny features
There are badgers, foxes and a hare
But to see them is very rare.

Gemma Kane (8)
Cygnet House Preparatory School, Bangor

Summer

S is for the sun
U is for under parasol relaxing
M is melting, our lollies are melting
M is for Michael and me playing beach ball
E is for excitement, we are going on holidays!
R is for rolling waves on the beach.

Laura McCreary (10)
Cygnet House Preparatory School, Bangor

School

The place that I love is school
And all my friends are so cool,
Some teachers are tall
But others are small,
They make us do work all day
But then we go out to play,
Some classes drive me round the bend
But here we go we've come to an end.

Grace Warwick (10)
Cygnet House Preparatory School, Bangor

Spring And Summer

Oh how I hate the winter
Oh how I hate the dark nights
Oh how I love the sight
Of spring and summer bright

Flowers bloom, stars gloom
A coloured crest in a nest
Grasses green, rivers stream
Farmers grow corn and baby animals are born.

Katie Lyall (8)
Cygnet House Preparatory School, Bangor

Winter

W is for winter one of our seasons.

I is for ice as cold as can be.

N is for night-time when Santa comes down the chimney.

T is for trees so bare with no leaves.

E is for excitement when you go to bed on Christmas Eve night

R is for rain which falls day and night.

Sophie Rowbotham (9)
Cygnet House Preparatory School, Bangor

Susan McCider

Susan McCider
Was a horse rider
She loved to jump
Even a tree stump
Africa her horse
Jumped a course
Crosses and straights
Barrels and crates
One day she fell off
Down into a water trough
So Susan McCider
Is no longer a horse rider.

Ashleigh Brimacombe (11)
Cygnet House Preparatory School, Bangor

My Name Is Molly

M is for Minxy, that's my nickname
O is for orange, that I love to eat
L is for laughing, that I love to do
L is for left-handed, the way I write and
Y is for yesterday, when I wrote this poem!

Molly McLarnon (7)
Cygnet House Preparatory School, Bangor

My Garden Fairy

There is someone living at the bottom of my garden
and no one knows but me
it is a very special secret
and I am as excited as can be.

For at the bottom of my garden
lives a fairy, Bluebell Rose
and she lives beneath a toadstool
where my mummy's flowers grow.

She flutters round the garden
when she sees me come out to play
and sprinkles round her fairy dust
so I will have a very magic day.

Bluebell Rose is very shy
so I can't let you see
where she lives beneath the toadstool
so her secret's safe with me.

Sophie Windebank (11)
Drumahoe Primary School, Londonderry

My Dog

My dog is called Ben.
He is white, cuddly and fluffy.
He has a little black nose.
He is a tiny dog.

I take my dog for walks.
He loves to play in the garden.
Ben is a good dog.
He's my only pet.

Andrew Crothers (11)
Drumahoe Primary School, Londonderry

The Next Big Step

The next big step will be a dread
So many new things will be whizzing through my head
Will all these classrooms look the same?
Will I remember the teachers' names?
Will they shout?
Will they yell?
Will I long to hear the bell?
But one thing's for sure
When it comes to September
Drumahoe School I'll miss you
Forever!

Lauren Hyndman (11)
Drumahoe Primary School, Londonderry

The Sky

The sky is lovely and blue,
Which we all know that's true,
Even the birds do too.

In the sky the sun shines bright,
The stars twinkle at night,
What a lovely sight.

Look at the sky, what a sight!
Just a pity about the height,
But we are happy tonight.

Samara Ritchie (11)
Drumahoe Primary School, Londonderry

Easter

Easter is a time of fun,
We're eating chocolate instead of buns,
The Easter bunny hopping along,
Singing, happily, his Easter song
And dancing proudly below the sun.

Fergus Gibson (11)
Drumahoe Primary School, Londonderry

Summer

When I am on holidays I have such fun,
Running and skipping in the sun.

While I am running across the beach,
I try to catch a butterfly while it's still in my reach.

When the weather is lovely and bright and sunny,
I listen to the bees buzzing as they make their honey.

As the day is coming to an end,
I wave goodbye to my warm sunny friend.

Holly Boyd (11)
Drumahoe Primary School, Londonderry

My Dog

I like the way
my dog looks,
he's white and
fluffy and round,
his legs are short
and he's very low to the ground.
He has two black eyes
and a black button nose
and they are the only things that show.
His eyes sparkle with glee
and shine with delight,
every time I come into sight.

Jill Jeffrey (11)
Drumahoe Primary School, Londonderry

I Like Football

I like football, what do you like?
I like Liverpool, who do you like?
I like Northern Ireland, who do you like?
I like Steven Gerrard, who do you like?
I like David Healy, who do you like?
I like all of these things, what about you?

Ethan Duddy (10)
Drumahoe Primary School, Londonderry

The Man From Londonderry

There once was a man from Londonderry
Who sailed away on a ferry
In the middle of the sea
He was stung by a bee
And fell overboard into the water.

The lifeboat plucked him from the ocean
They made him drink a magic potion
It made him turn green
Which caused a great scene
That was the end of the man from Londonderry.

Ryan Hetherington (11)
Drumahoe Primary School, Londonderry

Billy And Milly

There was an old man named Billy
Who had a pet called Milly
Milly was a cat
Who wore a top hat
Which looked really silly.

Rachel Montgomery (11)
Drumahoe Primary School, Londonderry

The Boy Wonder!

There was a boy called Dylan
Who liked to kick round a ball
Until he smashed his mum's lamp in the hall
'What have I told you?' she said
'I'll put that ball in the shed'
'She doesn't understand, if she'd leave me the way I am
I could be playing for West Ham
She might see me as being a fool
I'd show them all some day when I'm playing for Liverpool
You will be seeing me on TV
Scoring goals 1, 2, 3
Won't be worried about the stupid lamp then
Be just cheering me on.'

Dylan Craig (11)
Drumahoe Primary School, Londonderry

The Sea

The sea is a very old man.
He is stroppy and angry.
He dances like a penguin morning and night,
Even when he's tired he fights.
His eyes are as blue as the sky,
He watches you like a hawk.
His hair shimmers throughout the day,
He shouts like a grizzly bear.
Now he's calm, but for how long?

David McIntyre (10)
Glencraig Integrated Primary School, Holywood

The Sea

The sea was sloshing about.
It was roaring at the night sky.
The sea was running up the rocks.
The huge waves were going round and round,
Up and down, side to side.
I was out there on my boat when the waves came tumbling up.
I had quite a fright,
When I saw the crazy waves rolling up the boat.

Emma Shaw (11)
Glencraig Integrated Primary School, Holywood

The Moon

A shining orb of light,
A sparkly shimmering ball,
Lights up the darkest night,
The biting darkness set alight,
It glows so warmly through the night,
Holds back the clawing darkness,
Until it's done its job,
Assisted by the sparkling stars,
They rule the night sky,
A shining orb of light,
Is what we call the moon.

Harrison Ginn (11)
Glencraig Integrated Primary School, Holywood

The Volcano

The volcano was an angry giant shaking its fists.
Its voice roared like a lion.
Its red hair rushed like a cheetah.
Its eyes blazed like a fire.
Its nose was covered with bumps all ready to burst like boils.
Its guts boiled to explode.
The villagers underneath scared.
The trees shattered like a tired old man.

Stephanie Craig (11)
Glencraig Integrated Primary School, Holywood

One Night

One night I got such a fright,
When the rain started pounding on the window.
I ran outside to make sure it wasn't a dream,
When the rain pelted me on the shoulder.
I ran back inside and turned to shut the door,
To see the water creeping after me.
I shut the door and ran to the window,
To be met with the sight of dancing and bouncing on the car roof.
I ran back to bed and pulled up the covers,
But still I heard the raging roars on my skylight.
After what seemed like hours,
It fell to a spit every so often.
That night I had such a fright,
When the rain started pounding on the window.

Christopher Wright (11)
Glencraig Integrated Primary School, Holywood

The Sea

The swishing and splashing,
Twirling and dancing,
The sudden whoosh,
Spinning, crying, anguish and pain,
The sorrow and grief mourning for better treatment,
The dirt, the rubbish and the oil,
Spoiling him and making him rotten,
But make it a better place
And all will be forgotten.

Siona Davis (11)
Glencraig Integrated Primary School, Holywood

Snowflakes Falling

S wirling and twirling in the air,
N othing can stop them falling,
O ver the house and down the roof,
W ater is frozen with ice,
F alling faster and faster all the time,
L ayers of snow on the floor.
A ir is thick and cold,
K eep on falling so I can't go to school,
E veryone thinking about snow,
S wirling and twirling in the air.

F reezing snow and melting ice,
A ll bunched together floating,
L ying on the ground, for us to play with,
L uckily there's no school today,
I cicles pointy and sharp,
N othing can stop it falling,
G ardens are covered in a white sheet.

Victoria Duxbury (11)
Glencraig Integrated Primary School, Holywood

The Kitchen

The kitchen is a crazy place
Where things go wrong and messy
Sugar for salt, buns for beans
There're flies in my spaghetti
A cockroach in the pan
A tomato on the floor
The bread looks like a pancake.
Please don't give me more!

Jaime Anderson (11)
Glencraig Integrated Primary School, Holywood

The Television

The television lives in the corner,
Watching our every move.
It springs into life in the morning,
Calling loudly with the day's news.
It quietly dozes till evening,
When the channels flick to and fro.
News, music, cartoons or a film,
Perhaps singing from a musical show.
Silent again by nightfall,
His face so sombre and black.
So quiet and still now at bedtime,
No voices answering back.

Mark Crockford (11)
Glencraig Integrated Primary School, Holywood

The Rain

It dripped, it dropped
It pitter-pattered into the sea
Up into the clouds and whoosh, it fell
As it slipped and slithered
Down the mountains
Through the rivers
And it slowed down
Into the sea
And it glistened and shimmered
The whole night through.

Emily Hewitt (10)
Glencraig Integrated Primary School, Holywood

The Wind

The wind is very strong today.
Today it zoomed round the playground very fast.
It rushed through parks.
Trees fell on paths.
In gardens umbrellas tumbled.
Cushions flew up on roofs of houses.
Electricity lines fell on roads like whips.
Unlocked gates opened and closed.
Nuts and leaves fell from trees.

Hamish Mounsey (10)
Glencraig Integrated Primary School, Holywood

The Monstrous Sea

The sea is an angry monster
Waiting to attack.
It waved to me so I got in
Then it tossed me on my back.

I did not know where I was
It kept pulling me further out.
I watched as its waves crashed on the shore
And nobody heard my shout.

I swam and swam with all my might
But this monster was not giving up without a fight.
Then all of a sudden the anger ceased
The monster calmed and I was released.

Hannah King (11)
Glencraig Integrated Primary School, Holywood

The Volcano

The volcano was an angry giant shaking its fists.
Its voice roared, 'I'm coming to get you!'
Its red hair boiled away to nothing.
Its eyes looking down at the village it was going to get.
Its blood rushing down to eat the village.
Its teeth going to eat anything that came up its mountain.
Its arms wrapped around the island so no one could escape.
Its nose breathing in its lovely smoke.

Jamie Woods (10)
Glencraig Integrated Primary School, Holywood

The Great Fight

Like soldiers in a violent attack,
The raindrops battered the tent.
At first it was like machine-gun fire,
Then it changed as the wind gusted.
Deadly grenades of water and hailstones,
Pounded the sides of the flimsy canvas,
The explosions grew harder and harder,
As the waves of rain hit our position.
Everything inside the tent shook,
But we defended bravely until the assault ended.
And not one drop of enemy rain entered our camp.

David Cave (11)
Glencraig Integrated Primary School, Holywood

The Volcano

The volcano fizzed and oozed as he trudged through the city.
His face was glowing red with rage.
His eyes were gazing a fiery stare.
His arms crushed and mushed everything in his path.
His voice boomed and trembled with anger.
His legs grew longer as he stomped through the city.
His red hair rushed and hurried around.
His hands were burning with a fiery wrath.
The volcano fizzed and oozed as he trudged through the city.

David Duff (10)
Glencraig Integrated Primary School, Holywood

Hallowe'en

October 31st is here
The night of great fear.

I see the witches
Flying in their ditches.

I smell the smoke
From the big oak.

I taste the sweets
From all the trick or treats.

I feel the terrible pain
From the ghostly chain.

October 31st is gone
And is now the rise of dawn.

Jonathan O'Neill (10)
Kilmoyle Primary School, Ballymoney

I Like MiniMotos

I like
MiniMotos

The fast passing
Speedy kind

The rushing round
The track kind

The brightly painted
Looking kind

The cool designs
Shining in the sun kind

The really polished
Shiny kind

I do like
MiniMotos.

Mark Watters (10)
Kilmoyle Primary School, Ballymoney

Doctor Who

The Tardis lies in space
Going at the fastest pace

I see what no human will
And now know how Daleks kill

I hear a Dalek gun
And the explosion of the sun

I smell living plastic
Which is not fantastic

I taste horrible sweets
And fresh cut meats

All these are true
For I am Doctor Who.

William McCammond (10)
Kilmoyle Primary School, Ballymoney

Snow

Snow is white and soft
Snow is very cold
Snow is melting in my hand
It's very hard to hold

Snow is floating through the air
Snow is falling to the ground
On a cold and frosty night
Gliding gently all around

Snowballs flying through the air
And making men of snow
Snow can do a lot of things
I'm sure that you will know

Making ground quite slippery
Fields and mountains white
Sparkling on the rooftops
It is a beautiful sight.

Alison Montgomery (10)
Kilmoyle Primary School, Ballymoney

I Like Scramblers

I like scramblers
The class painted speedy kind
The fast passing kind
The big beast kind
The very heavy kind
Keeping your balance kind
The flying around the dirt track kind
The so cool kind
I do like scramblers.

Dylan Greer (10)
Kilmoyle Primary School, Ballymoney

Five Great Dogs

Five happy dogs
All wanted more
One took too much
And then there were four

Four silly dogs
Were playing with bees
One got stung
And then there were three

Three good dogs
Were playing with goo
One got stuck
And then there were two

Two fun dogs
Had too much fun
And one fell down
And then there was one.

Cameron Ashcroft (10)
Kilmoyle Primary School, Ballymoney

I Like Snow

I like snow
The shiver up your back kind
The pure white kind
The kind that makes you
Want to stay out all the time
The coldness in the air kind
The kind that makes you
Want to jump up and down
I do like snow!

Philip Richmond (11)
Kilmoyle Primary School, Ballymoney

My Favourite Mini Beasts

I like ladybirds
The colourful, pretty, spotty kind
The flying to a tree kind
Flying in the air
Landing on my fingers
I do like ladybirds.

I like butterflies
The colourful, pretty, lovely kind
The fluttering in the air kind
Running after them
So hard to catch
I do like butterflies.

Kathie Woodrow (9)
Kilmoyle Primary School, Ballymoney

Slugs And Butterflies

I like slugs
The slimy, slithery black kind
The slide along the ground kind
They move very slowly
Leaving a sticky, shiny trail
I do like slugs.

I like butterflies
The colourful, lovely, wonderful kind
The come up close to you kind
Try to grab them
Put them in a jar
I do like butterflies.

James Bleakly (10)
Kilmoyle Primary School, Ballymoney

Mini Beasts

I like spiders
The fat-bodied, juicy kind
The fast, quick, running kind
The big long-legged ones
The fastest ones
I do like spiders.

I like butterflies
The colourful, beautiful, lovely kind
The fluttery, flying kind
The flower-sucking
Colourful ones
I do like butterflies.

Jeff Purdy (10)
Kilmoyle Primary School, Ballymoney

The Tragedy Of England

This is the tragedy
Of when the England team fell ill
The week before they played Brazil

Paul Robinson was walking out his gate
Got hit by a bus
And will be out for eight

John Terry was going to see his brother Kevin
Walked into a manhole
And will be out for seven

Ashley Cole was lifting bricks
Five fell on him
So he'll be out for six

Frank Lampard had to dive
He broke his leg
And will be out for five

Joe Cole ran into a door
Broke his skull
And will be out for four

Wayne Rooney got stung by a bee
Ran round in circles
And will be out for three

Stevie G caught the flu
Fell out of bed
And will be out for two

Peter Crouch ate a bun
Found out it was poisonous
And will be out for one

That was the tragedy
When the England team fell ill
The week before they played Brazil.

David McKeeman (10)
Kilmoyle Primary School, Ballymoney

Terminators

(Inspired by 'Ten Naughty Schoolboys' by A A Milne)

Ten terminators all drinking wine
One malfunctioned
And then there were nine

Nine terminators climbing over a gate
One lost its head
And then there were eight

Eight terminators all going to Heaven
One didn't want to go
And then there were seven

Seven terminators all getting fixed
One exploded
And then there were six

Six terminators all feeling alive
One felt dead
And then there were five

Five terminators all wanting more
One had too much
And then there were four

Four terminators all at the sea
One fell in
And then there were three

Three terminators all shouted boo
One got scared
And then there were two

Two terminators all eating buns
One choked himself
And then there was one

One terminator sat on a gun
Pulled the trigger
And then there were none.

Jacob McAlister (11)
Kilmoyle Primary School, Ballymoney

Ten Jolly Ponies

(Inspired by 'Ten Naughty Schoolboys' by A A Milne)

Ten jolly ponies went in a line
One fell over
And then there were nine

Nine jolly ponies saw some bait
One got caught
And then there were eight

Eight jolly ponies went to Devon
One stayed there
And then there were seven

Seven jolly ponies had some ticks
One got bitten
And then there were six

Six jolly ponies saw a hive
One got stung
And then there were five

Five jolly ponies went into a store
The door came down
And then there were four

Four jolly ponies skipped around a tree
One hurt its knee
And then there were three

Three jolly ponies found some goo
One picked it up
And then there were two

Two jolly ponies saw a bun
One ate it
And then there was one

One sad pony had a gun
Shot itself
And then there were none.

Caroline Clarke (11)
Kilmoyle Primary School, Ballymoney

Christmas

Christmas Day is finally here
The happiest time of all the year.

I see a brightly lit Christmas tree
Children opening presents with glee.

I taste the delicious chocolate cake
On top there are crumbs of a flake.

I hear everyone laugh and shout
There will be much more noise, no doubt!

I touch the pines on the Christmas tree
Which was decorated by Annie, Ben and me.

Christmas Day was really great
And our guests didn't go home till late!

Abbie McIlhatton (10)
Kilmoyle Primary School, Ballymoney

Holidays

Holidays are finally here
Everyone is full of cheer.

I see people having fun
Children playing in the bright sun.

I hear children yelling with glee
Splashing each other in the sea.

I smell the burgers in the pan
Oh, it's too hot I need a fan.

I taste the ice cream in my mouth
The ice cream is very good in the south.

Robynne Blair (10)
Kilmoyle Primary School, Ballymoney

Famine

Ireland is hit by potato blight
For the people what a plight.

I see the starving people in the street
Trying to find something to eat.

I hear children screaming with fear
They no longer laugh with cheer.

I smell the rotting potatoes in the ground
If you touch them they make your hand go brown.

I taste the bland, rotting potatoes in my mouth
I wish we could travel to the south.

Emma Hartin (9)
Kilmoyle Primary School, Ballymoney

Snow

I remember snow glimmering in the winter sun,
What fun!

It may have been cold in the wintry air
But did we have a care?

Building a snowman was such fun
But who can stop at only one?

I remember snow.

Luke Watton Austin (11)
Kilmoyle Primary School, Ballymoney

The Famine

I hate the thought of the famine

Hunger, disease everywhere in the homes
No food leaves people like skin and bones
Money was so scarce
The great landlord so fierce

People have fled from here
But nowhere is there any good cheer
Little children, mums and dads
The whole family is very sad

I hate the thought of the hunger
In your belly it feels like thunder
The workhouse, the very worst thing
As you waken up a bell would ring

I hate the thought of the famine.

Matthew Steele (10)
Kilmoyle Primary School, Ballymoney

Six Happy Cats

(Inspired by 'Ten Naughty Schoolboys' by A A Milne)

Six happy cats
All saw a hive
One tried to get it
And then there were five

Five happy cats
All started to snore
One made the loudest
And then there were four

Four happy cats
Ran by the sea
One fell in
And then there were three

Three happy cats
Playing with a shoe
One got caught
And then there were two

Two happy cats
Had a cream bun
One got poisoned
And then there was one

One lonely cat
Had no fun
Went out for a run
And then there were none.

Dyan Sharkey (11)
Kilmoyle Primary School, Ballymoney

Chelsea V Manchester United

Carralho doing very well,
But then he tripped and fell.
Drogba got a belting goal,
Now it seems he is on a roll.
Man Utd equalised,
Rooney got penalised.
Lampard made it two-one,
For me, that was a lot of fun.
The full-time whistle goes,
Chelsea is best, Mr Ferguson knows.

Charlie Hayes (9)
Kilmoyle Primary School, Ballymoney

Snow

All around me I see snow,
I wonder if it will ever go.
As it flutters to the ground,
Listen! Not even a sound.
It is cold like a block of ice,
But do not eat it, it is not very nice.
It's soft, crunchy and fluffy too,
Whoops! I threw a snowball at you!

Janice Miskelly (11)
Kilmoyle Primary School, Ballymoney

Five Dancing Dogs

(Inspired by 'Ten Naughty Schoolboys' by A A Milne)

Five dancing dogs
Were eating an apple core
One choked himself
And then there were four

Four dancing dogs
Slept under a tree
One hit his head
And then there were three

Three dancing dogs
All went to the loo
One got flushed
And then there were two

Two dancing dogs
All went to the sun
One blew up
And then there was one

One dancing dog
Picked up a gun
Shot himself
And then there were none.

David Anderson (9)
Kilmoyle Primary School, Ballymoney

Five Swimming Goldfish

(Inspired by 'Ten Naughty Schoolboys' by A A Milne)

Five swimming goldfish
All wanting more
One ate too much
And then there were four

Four swimming goldfish
All swimming to me
One ate a stone
And then there were three

Three swimming goldfish
All going to chew
On ate a bug
And then there were two

Two swimming goldfish
All having fun
Sadly one died
And that left one

One lonely goldfish
All on its own
Always bored
And that leaves none.

John McLaughlin (9)
Kilmoyle Primary School, Ballymoney

The Magic Box

(Based on 'Magic Box' by Kit Wright)

I will put in my box . . .
A magic godmother so she would grant my every wish,
A touch of a snowflake on my tongue,
I would put in ten white doves.

I will put in the box . . .
The rustling of the trees at night,
A pack of magic cards,
A magic dice if you squeeze it sets a force field around you.

I will put in the box . . .
A magical clock that turns back time,
A magic golden egg that a dragon lives in,
A magic monkey if he farts or burps money comes out,
A big fat toe if you squeeze it magic dust comes out
and it makes you fly.

My box is fashioned from handbags, pencil sharpeners and eyes.

I shall swim the stormy ocean in my box,
I shall sun myself on the white sandy beaches.

Aoife McVeigh (10)
Laghey Primary School, Dungannon

Saturn

I'm one of the nine planets and Saturn is my name
You'd find me next to Jupiter if from the Earth you came
I'm most recognisable because of all my rings
But in this little poem I'll tell you more interesting things.

Although I am so massive and you think I would sink
I would actually float on water so I'm lighter than you think
My atmosphere is hydrogen with a little helium too
If you came to visit me it definitely wouldn't suit you.

The rings which I'm famous for are made of rock and ice
They're nicknamed Shepherd Satellites which I think is very nice
And as for moons, I've quite a lot, around about twenty-four
There's Titan and Mimas and Rhea and many, many more.

My days are short, my years are long, my surface very hot
I'm made of very thick gases, you'd like me not a lot
No running, jumping or dancing nor a place to build a school
No air to breathe, no water to fill the swimming pool.

Hope Bradley (11)
Loughries Primary School, Newtownards

The Red Planet

Round and round the sun we go
All nine planets in a row

So try and guess my name for fun
I'm 140 million miles and fourth from the sun

I get my name from the god of war
And you can't travel to me by car

Round and red, dry and dusty
They say my soil is very rusty

My night and temperatures are very cold
So only visit if you're daring and bold

My mountain range is my claim to fame
Olympus Mons, do you know it by name?

Phobos and Deimos are my two small moons
Up close my surface looks like orange sand dunes

To land on me would require a mask
As carbon dioxide makes up my main gas

Look for me amongst the stars
I give off a red glow and my name is Mars!

Rhys McKee (11)
Loughries Primary School, Newtownards

Neptune

Neptune is the god of the seas,
He likes to make a lot of breeze.
He makes the waves to ebb and flow,
He circles around the sun, moon and stars
And sometimes waves his hand at Mars.
Neptune is so very cold,
To go there one would be so bold.
Mars, Venus and Mercury all can be seen by the naked eye,
But not in the same place in the sky.
Your space shuttle can but fly
Past all the stars and by and by.
Neptune days are short on time,
And I can't think of another word to rhyme.

Anna McCormick (11)
Loughries Primary School, Newtownards

Venus

Venus is a very hot planet
Venus is hotter than Mercury
There is lots of lava on Venus
You would melt on Venus
Venus is one of the small planets
It is quite close to Earth and Mars.

Jack Ritchie (11)
Loughries Primary School, Newtownards

Pluto

My name is Pluto,
Round and round the sun I go,
Of all the planets I'm the smallest,
In fact I know I'm also the coldest.

A week in your world is a day in mine,
My moon Charon really likes to shine.
It puts me in the dark at night
And moves in the day to give me light.

Ross Deering (11)
Loughries Primary School, Newtownards

Uranus

My name is Uranus,
I'm the third biggest planet there is.
I'm slow and fun
As it takes me 84
Years to orbit the sun.
I was discovered by
William Herschel in 1781.I
As I'm very cold at -346 degrees,
I don't get much heat from the sun.

Samantha Paden (11)
Loughries Primary School, Newtownards

Happiness

Happiness is going to Blackpool.
Happiness is winning at football.
Happiness is ice cream on a sunny day.
Happiness is having friends.
Happiness is playing.
Happiness is a new CD.
Happiness is doing art.
Happiness is having good fun.
Happiness is being happy.

Eamonn O'Neill (8)
Lourdes Primary School, Whitehead

The Victorians

Victorians, Victorians, Victorians, Victorians
Astounding, magnificent, cunning Victorians
Smelly, smitten, sly Victorians
Imagining, inventing, achieving Victorians
Maid, mistress, master Victorians
Superior, inferior, snooty Victorians
Victorians, Victorians, Victorians, Victorians.

Claire Gault (11)
Rathmore Primary School, Bangor

Victorians

Victorians, Victorians, Victorians, Victorians
Cold, unhappy, unhealthy Victorians
Scruffy, sad, starving Victorians
Begging, scrounging, freezing Victorians
Miserable, meek, mourning Victorians
Victorians, Victorians, Victorians, Victorians.

Megan Wilson (10)
Rathmore Primary School, Bangor

Victorians, Victorians

Victorians, Victorians, Victorians, Victorians
Poor, rich, homeless Victorians
Streets, skirts, sick Victorians
Singing, walking, playing Victorians
Mines, medicine, modern Victorians
Tired, hungry, sad Victorians
Victorians, Victorians, Victorians, Victorians.

Xantia Quail-Mease (11)
Rathmore Primary School, Bangor

The Victorians

Victorians, Victorians, Victorians, Victorians
Hungry, poor, famine-washed Victorians
Strict, serious, secure Victorians
Inventing, working, cooking Victorians
Melancholy, musical, modest Victorians
Rich, well-fed, begging Victorians
Victorians, Victorians, Victorians, Victorians.

Darcy Richardson (11)
Rathmore Primary School, Bangor

The Victorians

Victorians, Victorians, Victorians, Victorians
Wicked, cruel, powerful Victorians
Sly, stout, short Victorians
Cunning, watching, thinking Victorians
Miserable, mistreated, mighty Victorians
Rich, dislikeable, devious Victorians
Victorians, Victorians, Victorians, Victorians.

Aaron Drury (11)
Rathmore Primary School, Bangor

The Victorians

Victorians, Victorians, Victorians, Victorians
Rich, disgusting, cold Victorians
Servant, shrivelled, screaming Victorians
Clothing, begging, starving, Victorians
Maids, maniac, masterly Victorians
Poor, disliked, ragged Victorians
Victorians, Victorians, Victorians, Victorians.

Amy Magee (10)
Rathmore Primary School, Bangor

The Victorians

Victorians, Victorians, Victorians, Victorians
Old, young, athletic Victorians
Sleepy, shattered, shameful Victorians
Working, running, playing Victorians
Mighty, mourned, melancholy Victorians
Tired, painful, dreaded Victorians
Victorians, Victorians, Victorians, Victorians.

Andrew Moore (10)
Rathmore Primary School, Bangor

Victorians

Victorians, Victorians, Victorians, Victorians
Thriving, prosperous, hard-working Victorians
Singing, sober, superior Victorians
Working, interesting, inventive Victorians
Modest, manufacturing, materialistic Victorians
Wealthy, smart, well-housed Victorians
Victorians, Victorians, Victorians, Victorians.

Colleen Magee (11)
Rathmore Primary School, Bangor

Victorians

Victorians, Victorians, Victorians, Victorians
Selfish, scruffy, skinny Victorians
Smart, slender, sweet Victorians
Stressing, making, sickly Victorians
Mucky, mischievous, mysterious Victorians
Delightful, revolting, sick Victorians
Victorians, Victorians, Victorians, Victorians.

Ben Crawford (11)
Rathmore Primary School, Bangor

The Victorians

Victorians, Victorians, Victorians, Victorians
Unfortunate, sad, poor Victorians
Sulky, scruffy, sullen Victorians
Begging, stinking, suffering Victorians
Mean, melancholy, mourned Victorians
Fortunate, happy, rich Victorians
Victorians, Victorians, Victorians, Victorians.

Erin Magee (11)
Rathmore Primary School, Bangor

The Victorians

Victorians, Victorians, Victorians, Victorians
Decorative, creative, inventive Victorians
Stealing, spanking, scolding Victorians
Starving, loathing, dying Victorians
Malnourished, moaning, moneyed Victorians
Loving, sharing, caring Victorians
Victorians, Victorians, Victorians, Victorians.

Jessica White (10)
Rathmore Primary School, Bangor

The Victorians

Victorians, Victorians, Victorians, Victorians
Sunday, singing songs Victorians
Singing, dancing, praising Victorians
Maids making magic Victorians
Victorians, Victorians, Victorians, Victorians.

Lucy Coyle (11)
Rathmore Primary School, Bangor

The Victorians

Victorians, Victorians, Victorians, Victorians
Richer, deficient, unfortunate Victorians
Swine, servants, sitting room Victorians
Drawing room, cooking, singing Victorians
Mature, miner, mirror Victorians
Beautiful, gorgeous, ravishing Victorians
Victorians, Victorians, Victorians, Victorians.

Sarah Heath (10)
Rathmore Primary School, Bangor

The Victorians

Victorians, Victorians, Victorians, Victorians
Filthy, grimy, grubby, Victorians
Suffering, shivering, snivelling Victorians
Revolting, disgusting, nauseating Victorians
Miserable, melancholic, mournful Victorians
Vile, foul, nasty Victorians
Victorians, Victorians, Victorians, Victorians.

Jack Denny (11)
Rathmore Primary School, Bangor

The Victorians

Victorians, Victorians, Victorians, Victorians
Wealthy, selfish, greedy, Victorians
Snobby, sick, sedate Victorians
Thriving, boring, fun-loving Victorians
Money-loving, manipulating, money-haggling Victorians
Vile, vicious, bland Victorians
Victorians, Victorians, Victorians, Victorians.

Melissa Lynn (11)
Rathmore Primary School, Bangor

The Victorians

Victorians, Victorians, Victorians, Victorians
Cold, dark, scary Victorians
Study, saints, in school Victorians
Age of steam opened a dream for Victorians
Inventing, exploring, travelling Victorians
Excited, kind, revolutionary Victorians
Victorians, Victorians, Victorians, Victorians.

Campbell Baker (10)
Rathmore Primary School, Bangor

The Victorians

Victorians, Victorians, Victorians, Victorians
Posh, flamboyant, distinguished Victorians
Smelly, spiteful, sordid Victorians
Disgusting, coughing, stealing Victorians
Malicious, macabre, mad Victorians
Fantastic, lovely, eccentric Victorians
Victorians, Victorians, Victorians, Victorians.

Conor Wright (11)
Rathmore Primary School, Bangor

The Crocodile

The crocodile's eyes are two mud piles stacked onto the ground,
His nose is two little holes in the wall,
His teeth are like butcher knives, just been sharpened,
And his tail is a long and never-ending road.

The crocodile's skin is like the bark of a tree, which has
been living for years,
His claws are very slimy, tiny pads,
His dark mouth is like a red mat,
And his nails are thorns sticking out of a bush.

The crocodile's smell is horrible, it's like milk which has
gone off for a year,
His touch is like tiny pebbles covered with moss,
His mood is a dark, dreary Hallowe'en night,
And his head shape is an ice cream cone.

Sophie Holland (11)
St Colmcilles Primary School, Downpatrick

Koala Bear

Koala bear's eyes are like stretched black buttons,
His noise is a miniature bell,
His ears are like tiny cute curves
And his claws are my longest witches' nails.

Koala bear's body is like my small PE bag stuffed up
His arms are baby-soft and as short as can be,
His legs are like big fat sausages
And his sound is as silent as swimming swans.

Koala bear's fur is like the softest cloud in the sky,
His hands are podgy babies' hands,
His feet are like fluffed-out cotton balls
And his head is a little bag of apples bashed into place.

Chloe Kelly (10)
St Colmcilles Primary School, Downpatrick

The Husky Dog

Husky dog's fur is as white as a sheep's wool.
His tail is bigger than a snake.
His teeth are as sharp as the Grim Reaper's scythe
And his eyes are two disco balls.

Husky dog's bark sounds like he's being strangled.
His claws are sharper than a chainsaw.
His paws are like a pair of mittens
And his ears are two hearing detectors.

Husky dog's tongue is like a slithering eel.
His nose is a snout carrier.
His breath smells like a stinky skunk.
And his behaviour is terrible.

Jamie Dinsdale
St Colmcilles Primary School, Downpatrick

An American Grizzly Bear

Grizzly bear's eyes are like two lumps of coal.
His teeth are the ends of arrows.
His paws are puffy balls
And his fur is brown and silky.

Grizzly bear is as smart as a human.
His nose is a little black pebble.
His ears are two little brown silky balls
And he smells like dead fish lying for weeks.

Grizzly bear sounds like a howling wolf.
His height is as tall as a bean pole growing for five years.
His nails are as sharp as needles
And his eyebrows are all bushy and silky.

Shannon Lavery (10)
St Colmcilles Primary School, Downpatrick

The Polar Bear

Polar bear's eyes are like bright stars in the night,
His claws are witches' fingernails,
His paws are like soft red cushions
And his fur is sheep's wool.

Polar bear's teeth as sharp as razors,
His ears are round circles,
His nose is squashed as a button
And his mouth is an open purse.

Polar bear's roar is a beating drum,
His smell is like dog breath,
His taste is a fish finger
And his tail is round as a ball.

Michelle Blaney
St Colmcilles Primary School, Downpatrick

The Fox

The fox's eyes are like burning fires on a winter night,
His tail is a bending brush that sways in the moonlight,
His teeth are like jagged icicles on the top of a cave
And his fur is a sleek, smooth velvet cushion.

The fox's smell is like rotten food in a compost bin,
His sound is hailstones falling, pitter-patter along the ground,
His claws are like pointed pencil leads sticking into you
And his nose is a rotten wet potato.

The fox's whiskers are like thin, springy violin strings,
His legs are pipe cleaners, skinny but strong,
His ears are like two-way radios that pick up any sound
And his paws are like foam balls that bounce when he walks.

Grainne Gleeson (11)
St Colmcilles Primary School, Downpatrick

The Jaguar

The jaguar's spots are like dark grey clouds on a stormy night.
His whiskers are long, thin guitar strings.
His eyes are like orange spotlights lined with dark, thick eyeliner
And his ears are like halved peaches.

The jaguar's mouth is like a red and white trapdoor.
His tail is a long spotted snake.
His paws are light, fluffy pink cotton buds or pink clouds
And his claws are pins and needles.

The jaguar's fangs are as big as javelin sticks.
His coat is the desert plains covered in dirt and coal.
His tongue is like a flattened red ball covered in water
And his nose is a wet, cold black butterfly.

Nicole Clinton (10)
St Colmcilles Primary School, Downpatrick

Rottweiler

Rottweiler's eyes are the clouds in the moonlight,
His colour is black and tan,
His fur is a flat black road
And his tail is a round black ball.

Rottweiler's lick is like having a bottle of water thrown on you,
His teeth are as sharp as razor blades,
His mouth is a puddle of water
And his paws are small soft pillows.

Rottweiler's smell is a cinnamon stick,
His bark is a car crash,
His ears are short floppy sleepers
And his collar is camouflage-green.

Niall Clinton (10)
St Colmcilles Primary School, Downpatrick

Rhino

Rhino's eyes are as black as coal,
His teeth are leaves, flat and thin,
His skin is like mud, dry and rough
And his tail is a snake, small and flexible.

Rhino's horn is a giant pin, sharp and strong,
His foot is a fist fierce and wide,
His smell is like a swamp, foul and filthy
And his sound is a grunt, a cry for help.

Rhino's paws are like hammers, heavy and smooth,
His tongue is a fire, red and bright,
His legs are like trees, thick and strong
And his ears are flowers round and long.

Scott Stringer (11)
St Colmcilles Primary School, Downpatrick

Penguin

Penguin's coloured feathers are Jaffa Cakes,
His beak is like a black shell,
His feet is a black ground
And his eyes are like dark coal.

Penguin's face is a small black bag,
His arms are like big jellyfish,
His tail is a floppy rubber
And he sounds like a big chicken.

Penguin's neck is a small sun,
His stomach is soft like snow,
His back is a big black bin
And he moves like a brown snail.

Rebecca Curran (10)
St Colmcilles Primary School, Downpatrick

The Swan

Swan's feathers are like flames of love floating on water.
His eyes are shiny buttons nicely set into place.
His small feathers are like clouds all fluffed and puffed
And his beak is the top of a yacht setting sail.

Swan's body is like a romantic love boat at sea.
His neck is a fine number seven.
His feet are like flippers floating about
And his head a tiny pouch, nodding up and down.

Swan's colour is a passionate white.
His sound is like a silent ripple.
His legs are little candlesticks floating gently
And his wings are like an angel's flight.

Natasha Fitzsimons (10)
St Colmcilles Primary School, Downpatrick

The Lion

Lion's eyes are like a thunderstorm,
His ears are thin and spaghetti hoops,
His teeth are like thorns being pulled out from his skin
And his tail is as soft as padded cushions.

His smell is like a dead fish,
His sound is a loud horror movie,
His feet are like sticky marshmallows
And his fur is a mink coat.

His claws are as sharp as dragon daggers,
His nose is like a big pointy hat,
His whiskers are thin as burnt chips
And his mane is like a hairy werewolf.

Sean McGuigan (11)
St Colmcilles Primary School, Downpatrick

The German Shepherd Dog

The German shepherd dog's smell is like sour milk,
His paws are scrunchy as marshmallows,
His claws are like a sharp steak knife
And his eyes are as round as a full moon.

The dog's nose is black as a blackboard,
His fur is like a Pot Noodle,
His ears are as floppy as a spring
And his feet are as long as a metre stick.

The dog's legs are as long as an elephant's trunk,
His teeth are like witches' nails,
His breath smells like a dead fish
And his tail is like a broken lead.

Connie O'Shea (10)
St Colmcilles Primary School, Downpatrick

A Hamster

Hamster's eyes are as black as a blackboard,
His teeth are pegs on the washing line,
His ears are like very small buttons
And his tail is a small broken lead.

Hamster's hair colour is like rabbits', brown,
His feet are soft cotton wool rolled up,
His smell is like a dump yard
And his paw nails are sharp drawing pins.

Hamster's nose is like a lump of glitter,
His behaviour is a dunk woman on a Saturday night,
His back legs are small like cut-up card,
His front legs are like long blunt pencils.

Cillian Hughes
St Colmcilles Primary School, Downpatrick

The Dog Junior

Dog's eyes are brown as mud,
His teeth are sharp razor blades,
His ears are as furry as mats
And his smell is a dirty dumpster.

Dog's tail is as fluffy as cotton wool,
His sound is a loud screaming noise,
His claws are like small talons
And his feet are as thin as string.

Dog's coat is like wet noodles,
His paws are puffy pillows,
His size is like a giant
And his whiskers are long, thin laces.

Thomas Leavy (11)
St Colmcilles Primary School, Downpatrick

My Favourite Things

I like my friends
They are so cool
I like PlayStation
It is a great tool
Sunny days make me smile
And I love to run a mile
Rock music is the best
Better than all the rest
Hip hip hooray for a lovely day
What else can I say?

Ciaran McMenamin (7)
St Joseph's School, Crossgar

School

I go to school every day.
I like to go outside and play.
My favourite subject it is maths
And when I do the tests I pass.
I love it when we go to art,
Painting is my favourite part;
And then when we go out for PE,
There are lots of things to see.
My teachers they are very kind
And all the children too;
And if I didn't have a school,
I don't know what I'd do!

Leah McKeown (7)
St Laurence O'Toole's Primary School, Belleeks

My Birthday

I am seven today,
My friends are coming to my house to play.
We will play 'pass the parcel',
'Musical chairs' and 'musical statues'.
We will have drinks and a cake
And sandwiches and crisps and tray bakes.
With lots of presents just for me,
We will all be full of glee.

Fainche Quinn (7)
St Laurence O'Toole's Primary School, Belleeks

My Auntie's Dog

I have an aunt, she lives far away,
I go and visit her for a day.
She has a big dog with six little puppies,
I once lifted one and it was soft and fluffy.
The dog is called Sheba, she is brown and grey,
I may get a puppy one day.
They play together and have fun in the sun.
Can I have a puppy, just two, just one?

Cathal Doran (7)
St Laurence O'Toole's Primary School, Belleeks

My Best Friend

My best friend Lee
Is very nice to me.
He is a little busy bee.
In our garden he broke a tree
And ran as far as I could see.
My friend Lee!

Patrick McVerry (7)
St Laurence O'Toole's Primary School, Belleeks

My Dog

I have a dog called Billy,
He is ever so silly.
He likes to run, and have some fun
And play with our cat called Milly.

Ryan Kelly (7)
St Laurence O'Toole's Primary School, Belleeks

School

Oh why do we have school?
It isn't as if it's cool.
What's with science?
Just pay me some allowance.
We shouldn't go to maths
So please take me out of class!
And homework!
What do you think I am?
I'd rather put on pink lip balm.
I'd rather swim in a mucky dam,
I'd even rather pretend to have an imaginary friend called Sam!
So answer this all the teachers - why do we have to go to school?

Fearghus Quinn (10)
St Laurence O'Toole's Primary School, Belleeks

My Sister

I have a sister,
Her name is Grace.
She lives in Heaven,
It's a special place.

We have a cousin,
Her name is Megan.
She also lives up
In Heaven.

They play all day
And shine all night.
A beautiful star
Ever so bright.

P J Carroll (9)
St Laurence O'Toole's Primary School, Belleeks

My Dog

My dog Spike is white.
He is summer.
He is in a garden.
A clear sunny day.
He is a bright red shirt.
He is a leather chair.
He is a holiday programme.
He is a hot curry.
He is like a spiky hedge.
He is my dog, Spike.

Ronan Fearon (10)
St Oliver Plunkett's Primary School, Armagh

A Treacherous Cat

A treacherous monster is the cat.
Once it looks you'd better run
Because it has a very dangerous bite.
Do not be fooled
A cat is a killing machine.
This cat will not stop
Until it kills you.
Its fluffy tail will slash your legs off
So watch out!

Aaron Hughes (11)
St Oliver Plunkett's Primary School, Armagh

My Bike

My bike is as big as a house,
Its wheel is like an ocean.
My bike is fast when it is in motion.
My bike is as fast as a shooting star.
My bike is light and it flies like a kite.

Fionntan Nixon (11)
St Oliver Plunkett's Primary School, Armagh

My Mum

My mum is as bright as a button.
She shines like a star glowing in the sky.
She is as warm as the sun.
She is as cuddly as a teddy bear.

My mum is like a bright yellow T-shirt.
She smells like a big bunch of flowers.
She is as hot as the oven and bakes lovely muffins.

Patricia McKeever (10)
St Oliver Plunkett's Primary School, Armagh

The Vikings

When the Vikings settle in,
You will find they will always win!
Their boats are light and swift,
They can easily lift.
The monks are terrified of this race,
They think that they are a disgrace.
Vikings are not full of honesty,
When they raid the monastery.
The Vikings are full of pleasure,
When they have the treasure.

Eoghan McAtarsney (10)
St Oliver Plunkett's Primary School, Armagh

Homework

I have to do my homework,
I don't like it at all.
My daddy has to check it,
It drives him up the wall.

I learn a lot of science,
About birds and plants and trees,
But my favourite is the body,
About eyes and ears and knees.

I have to do a pile of maths,
It doesn't make much sense.
It's full of funny units,
Like grams and litres and pence.

That brings me to the English,
It takes up so much time.
I've read a lot of verses,
In poems that do not rhyme.

Sarah McCaw (11)
St Oliver Plunkett's Primary School, Armagh

A Hot Curry

Out of the oven,
Into my mouth.
I taste that
Hot, hot curry.
It is as hot
As the sun.

Before I have
Another bite,
I have to have a drink.
An icy cold drink,
So different to a
Hot, hot curry.

I can hear the ice-cold water.
I can smell the hot, hot curry.
I can touch the fork,
But the best thing of all
I can taste the hot, hot curry.

Laura Williamson (11)
St Oliver Plunkett's Primary School, Armagh

My Cat

My cat is bright black and bright white,
She is a nice warm pillow,
She is a field of flowers,
She is spring,
She is a clear sunny day,
She is a bright blue shirt,
She is a nice armchair,
She is a best-selling programme,
She is the biggest apple pie and custard ever.
My cat is a bit fat and she likes to eat bats and rats,
She likes lying on my bed like she is dying,
She has four mittens and she's had four kittens.

James Bown (10)
St Oliver Plunkett's Primary School, Armagh

My Friend

I once had a friend
Who pushed me down
And stole my milk money.
He chased me about.
My toy was broken,
I know who did it,
It did not take long to think.
I once had a friend,
Who was not a friend at all.

John-Joe Fearon (11)
St Oliver Plunkett's Primary School, Armagh

My Dog

My dog is lazy
Weak and fat
He has a brown, lovely coat
Like a chestnut cap.

He is lazy, so lazy
But produce a ball
And watch him jump alert
And he will crawl.

But when I go to bed
He will rattle about
And wreck the house.

But would I swap him for anything
In the world? No! No!
I would not
I would not
Ever.

Kathleen Courtney (9)
St Oliver Plunkett's Primary School, Armagh

My Daddy Is The Headmaster

My daddy has rules, he embarrasses me!
They are:
No spitting, no chewing, no fun you see.
No music, no jewellery, no make-up, no telly
And no big bellies.
No rude noises, no videos, no football,
Oh what a boring school this is.
No coloured socks, nor no PE
No jeans, no smiling, no gum
You are not allowed to wipe bogeys
                    down the side of the chair.
No breathing air.
All types of things like that you know.
I wish he'd keep these things until home time.

Eimear Murray (11)
St Oliver Plunkett's Primary School, Armagh

The Deep-Sea Diver

Billy is a diver,
A deep-sea diver,
Billy is a diver,
At nine years old.
Billy finds a treasure chest,
A treasure chest,
Billy finds a treasure chest,
At ten years old.
Billy is a boxer,
A big strong boxer,
Billy is a boxer
At eleven years old.
Billy is a rich boy,
With a thousand dollar bill,
Billy is a rich boy,
At twelve years old.

Conor McGlinchey (9)
St Oliver Plunkett's Primary School, Armagh

Hot Curry

When you go to a Chinese,
You give your order
And say, 'Please

I want a curry,
Nice and hot.
Please do not worry,
It's going in the pot.'

Sitting at home,
It's on the plate.
Eating alone,
Won't share with my mate!

Michael Gwynne (11)
St Oliver Plunkett's Primary School, Armagh

The Little Horse

The sun is rising over the hilltops
Hits the field
The young horse awakes

He gets up
And then falls as a raindrop
His mother comes over
And helps him walk

The little horse can walk and run
He comes and nuzzles
And lies down to bask in the weak sun

It's getting late and cold
He's sleepy and moves away
His mother comes over
Smiling proudly at her little boy

I come over the next day
He is not there
Oh no, where did he go?
Taken away, stolen or lost

I look over, I see something
It's him the little horse!
He looks at me as if he were mine

My father says, 'Come to me
That horse is yours, you see.'

Chloe Hughes (10)
St Oliver Plunkett's Primary School, Armagh

Winter

The winter is a caring mother.
She is frosty and kind.
Her face is like Jack Frost.
Her eyes are like leaves of holly.
Winter's coat is made of cold icicles and fluffy snow.
Her hair is like a falling red juicy berry.
Her pockets are full of joy and happiness.
She lives in an igloo with Jesus.
I love Winter.
She makes me feel like I am safe.

Chelsea Burrows (8)
Silverstream Primary School, Greenisland

Winter

The winter is a happy grandma.
She is icy and shiny.
Her face is like a soft snowflake.
Her eyes are like cold icicles.
Winter's coat is made of fluffy snowflakes
                         and shiny icicles.
Her hair is soft and long.
Her pockets are full of money and snowballs
                         and frosty berries.
She lives in ice and frost.

Tammy-Lee Johnston (8)
Silverstream Primary School, Greenisland

Winter

The winter is my mum.
Her face is like soft and shiny snow.
Her eyes are like red berries.
Her coat is made of cold ice.
Her hair is made of snowflakes.
Her pockets are full of toys.
She lives up north with a pet bear.
I like Winter.
She makes me feel kind like her.

Rhiannon McFadden (8)
Silverstream Primary School, Greenisland

Winter

The winter is a happy boy.
He is kind and helpful.
His face is like snow.
His eyes are like snowflakes.
Winter's coat is made of snow, fluffy stuff
        and frosty stuff like berries on trees.
His hair is soft like snow.
His pockets are full of toys, snowmen and
                money for Christmas presents.
He lives in Carrick with his mum, dad, dog and sister.
I like Winter!
He makes me feel happy and he is funny.
He's like snowflakes on your nose.

Hannah Cardwell (8)
Silverstream Primary School, Greenisland

Winter

The winter is a nice kind dad.
He is frosty, shiny and posh.
His face is like a snowflake gleaming.
His eyes are as white as snow.
Winter's coat is made of white animals' fluffy fur
                        and a bit of animal skin.
His hair is brown with splinters.
His pockets are full of cold and snow and snowflakes.
He lives in a cottage in the forest with his
                        wife, son and daughter.
I love Winter.
Winter makes me feel happy, joyful and proud.

Ben Tosh (8)
Silverstream Primary School, Greenisland

Winter

The winter is magic like Santa.
He is happy on his sleigh.
His face is cream peaches.
His eyes are hazel, like a hazelnut.
Winter's coat is made of joy, happiness and fun.
His pockets are full of candy canes and toys.
He lives in an old cottage with the reindeer.
I love Winter.
He makes me feel special.

William Gray (8)
Silverstream Primary School, Greenisland

Winter

The winter is happy boys.
He is going out to play.
His face is like snow and ice.
His eyes are like snow and stuff.
Winter's coat is made out of fluff like snow,
And his frosty coat is like berries on a tree.
His hair is as soft as snow.
His pockets are full of snowballs and money
                              for Xmas time.
He lives in Belfast with his mum and dad.
I like Winter.
He makes me feel so soft.

Nathan Blackwood (9)
Silverstream Primary School, Greenisland

Winter

The winter is an old granny shouting over shopping.
Her face is like a red berry.
Her eyes are like a stunning blue plate.
Winter's coat is made of frosty snowflakes and
                                    shiny icicles.
Her hair is like Santa's fluffy bear.
Her pockets are full of berries, shiny icicles
                              and snowflakes.
She lives in my house with her reindeer.
I hate Winter.
She makes me feel very, very weird.

PJ Moth (8)
Silverstream Primary School, Greenisland

Winter

The winter is Jesus.
He is kind and loving and he saved us.
His face is like soft snow.
His eyes are as blue as crystals.
Winter's coat is made of fur and fluffy wool.
His hair is as soft as a blanket.
His pockets are full of love and thoughtful 'thinkings'.
He lives in Heaven - a cold place with frosty snow.
I love Winter.
He makes me feel loving and caring.

Abbie Johnston (7) & Noel Hartley (9)
Silverstream Primary School, Greenisland

Winter

The winter is a snow monster.
He is icy and fluffy.
His face is like a frosty moon.
His hair is the golden stars.
His pockets are full of snowflakes
                    and a gust of wind.
He lives in a snow cave with
                    six dogs and a wife.
I like Winter.
He makes me feel happy.

Dean Cromie (9)
Silverstream Primary School, Greenisland

Little Brother Winter

The winter is a funny, happy brother.
His face is cheerful, kind and helpful.
His face is like a little snowman.
His eyes are as blue as the sky.
Winter's coat is made of fluffy snowflakes
                        and shiny icicles.
His hair is as blond as wheat in a field.
His pockets are full of happiness and joy,
                        and keys and sweets.
He lives in an ice castle.
I like Winter.
He makes me feel happy.

Ethan Morrow (8)
Silverstream Primary School, Greenisland

Miss Claus

The winter is Miss Claus.
She is soft and fluffy.
Her face is like lovely soft cream.
Her eyes are like a crystal shade of blue.
Winter's coat is made of fluffy feathers
                    and soft cold icicles.
Her hair is fluffy fur.
Her pockets are full of money and tissues.
She lives in the North Pole with reindeer.
I love Winter.
She makes me feel happy.

Amy Nicholson (8)
Silverstream Primary School, Greenisland

Winter

The winter is Mr Who.
He is cold and icy.
His face is like ice.
His eyes are coal.
Winter's coat is made of shiny ice
  and soft snow and coal for buttons.
His hair is shiny ice.
His pockets are full of candy and
                keys for his snow home.
He lives in the snow with a snow cat.
I like Winter.
He makes me feel happy.

Craig Manning (8)
Silverstream Primary School, Greenisland

Young Writers Information

We hope you have enjoyed reading this book - and that you will continue to enjoy it in the coming years.

If you like reading and writing poetry drop us a line, or give us a call, and we'll send you a free information pack.

Alternatively if you would like to order further copies of this book or any of our other titles, then please give us a call or log onto our website at www.youngwriters.co.uk

**Young Writers Information
Remus House
Coltsfoot Drive
Peterborough
PE2 9JX**

(01733) 890066